Department of the Environment
Ancient Monuments and Historic Buildings

Old Wardour Castle

WILTSHIRE

History by
R. B. PUGH MA, FSA
Formerly Editor, Victoria History of the Counties of England

Description by
A. D. SAUNDERS MA, FSA
Chief Inspector of Ancient Monuments and Historic Buildings

LONDON: HER MAJESTY'S STATIONERY OFFICE

First published 1968
Fifth impression 1978

ISBN 0 11 670305 9

Contents

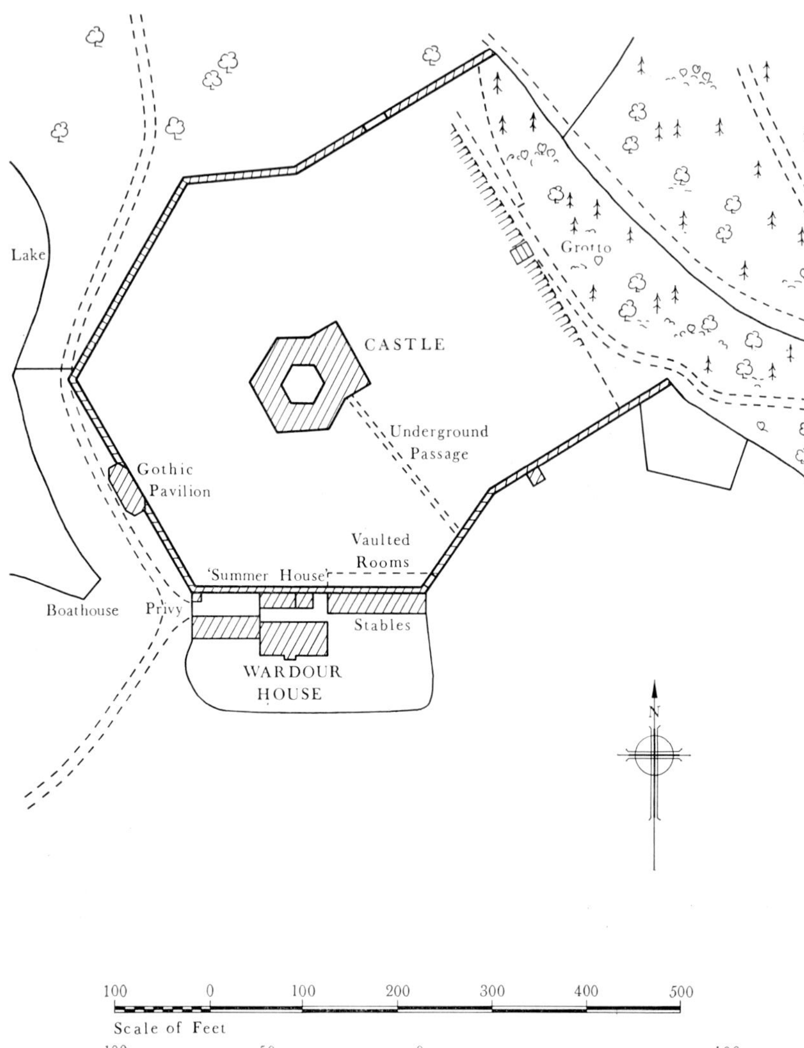
Lake
Gothic
Pavilion
CASTLE
Underground
Passage
Grotto
Vaulted
Rooms
'Summer House'
Boathouse
Privy
Stables
WARDOUR
HOUSE
N
100 0 100 200 300 400 500
Scale of Feet
100 50 0 100
Scale of Metres

History

THE OWNERS OF WARDOUR

The manor or village of Wardour is first mentioned by name in a document of the late ninth century. The document tells us that King Alfred delivered judgement in a dispute "while he stood washing his hands within the chamber there." It does not seem unlikely that the chamber in which the King acted with such nonchalance was in his own house and that Wardour was consequently a royal manor at the time. When at the end of William the Conqueror's reign the "description of England" called Domesday Book was compiled, the manor is found in the hands of Wilton Abbey, a house of Benedictine nuns some 10 miles (16km) away to the east. Since this was a monastery that greatly benefited from royal favours, it is possible, if the foregoing surmise is correct, that the Conqueror, Cnut, or even Alfred himself gave Wardour to it. With Wilton Abbey the overlordship remained until at least 1523 and probably until the Dissolution.

By 1086 the Abbess of Wilton had entrusted the manor to an undertenant called Britmar, of whom nothing further is known. By 1200 Britmar had been succeeded by Geoffrey de St Martin, and with the St Martin family Wardour remained until the death of Sir Lawrence de St Martin in 1385. Lawrence left as heirs two nephews, by one of whom, Thomas Calston, Wardour was inherited. By a process now seemingly impossible to trace, the manor had, by 1393, descended to John, fifth Lord Lovel, who was given leave in that year to "crenellate" or fortify his house there and make a castle of it. Lovel's ancestors had once possessed a fortified manor house at Titchmarsh in Northamptonshire, but by 1363 the building was ruinous. Possibly Lovel remembered this house in its days of glory, wished to reproduce it on Wiltshire soil, and consequently petitioned for the licence.

William, Lord Lovel, the builder's grandson, succeeded to the property, and his son John, seventh Lord Lovel, after him. The latter, however, sided with the Lancastrians in 1460 and in consequence lost many of his lands on Edward IV's accession. Some of these were indeed later restored to him but Wardour was not among them. For many years after this different owners or occupiers follow one another in fairly rapid succession. John Tuchet, Lord Audley, was made keeper of the castle in 1461 and again in 1478. Between his custodies the castle was held for a few months by William Neville, Earl of Kent, and after him by the King's brother George, Duke of Clarence, from 1463 to 1478. By 1486 it had come into the hands of Thomas Butler, Earl of

Ormond, who settled it for life upon Sir John Cheyne, created Lord Cheyne in 1487. When Cheyne died in 1499 it returned to Ormond, who at once sold it to Robert, Lord Willoughby de Broke, whose mother was a Cheyne. He owned it throughout his life and so did his son, the second baron, who was also called Robert.

The second Lord Broke married twice. By his first wife he had one son who died in his father's lifetime leaving three daughters; by his second he had three sons and two daughters. According to the strict rules of succession the property should at Lord Broke's death have been divided equally between his three grand-daughters by his first marriage. Some contemporaries claimed, however, that Lord Broke had set the normal rules aside and instead made a will by which he left the property to the sons (or some of them) by the second marriage subject to the interest, until death or remarriage, of his second wife. Others said that the first Lord Broke had settled the property upon his younger sons Sir Anthony and Nicholas Willoughby.

Exactly what the rightful succession was will perhaps never be known. It is certain that Elizabeth, a daughter of the second baron's sister by his first marriage, was put in possession of the property in 1530. She had by that time married Fulk Greville and later became Baroness Willoughby de Broke in her own right. Upon these two the property was settled in 1537. By 1539 Elizabeth's sister, Blanche, who was married to Sir Francis Dawtrey, also seems to have acted as though she and her husband owned a part of the property, though their rights, if any, are not otherwise heard of. On the other hand, at the very time when the settlement upon the Grevilles was being made, Sir Anthony Willoughby was granting leases of the property as though he were the landlord.

It was no doubt in the hope of disentangling the rival family claims that an action was begun in the Star Chamber about 1532, but if judgement was ever delivered it is not known what form it took. In the end, in 1541 and 1544, Anthony Willoughby and his son surrendered whatever interest they had to the Grevilles, who, thus safely entrenched, sold the property in 1547 to Sir Thomas Arundell of Lanherne, a Cornish village not far from Newquay. The purchaser, however, was convicted of felony in 1552 and forfeited all his lands. Wardour was then bought, though without vacant possession, by William Herbert, Earl of Pembroke.

It has been mentioned that in the thirties and forties both Anthony Willoughby and the Grevilles made leases of the castle. The names of

View of the castle across the lake

the lessees are not without interest, since it was presumably they and not the landlords who were or hoped to be occupiers. One of Anthony Willoughby's tenants was no less a person than Henry Courtenay, Marquess of Exeter, but two years after the lease was made he was executed for high treason and forfeited all his goods including the lease. The Grevilles' tenant of 1541 was a William Grinston of Motcombe in Dorset. By 1546 he had been succeeded by Matthew Colthurst, auditor of the Court of Augmentations in the south-western counties and therefore a business associate of the Arundell family. After Matthew's death Lawrence Hyde, grandfather of the first Lord Clarendon (died 1674), married his widow and succeeded to the tenancy. He was living in the castle in 1568 and was still tenant two years later. With him the succession of tenants ends, for in 1570 Sir

An eighteenth-century drawing of the main front (in the possession of Mr J Arundell)

Matthew Arundell, son of the purchaser in 1547, bought the property back from Lord Pembroke's son and eight years later began to reconstruct the castle.

Matthew's son Thomas inherited the castle in 1592. Three years later he distinguished himself in war by capturing the Turkish standard at the siege of Gran in Hungary. The Emperor Rudolf II thereupon made him a Count of the Holy Roman Empire and in 1605 James I raised him to the peerage as Baron Arundell of Wardour. From that time castle, manor, and park descended with the barony. The descent was only broken once, when under an Act of Parliament of 1652, the third baron forfeited his property for his adherence to the Royalist cause. Nearly all his lands, however, were bought by a friend and resold to their former owner at the Restoration.

The last Lord Arundell died in 1944. R J A Talbot, a grandson of the ninth baron through the female line, then succeeded to the property and took the name Arundell. His son, Mr R J R Arundell, now owns it. In 1936 the castle was placed in the guardianship of what is now the Department of the Environment.

During the period in which the penal laws were in force, the Arundells were one of the leading recusant families in England. In the first Lord Arundell's time there was a Roman Catholic chapel in the castle and during the seventeenth century Roman Catholic chaplains often resided with the family. One such was present during the first siege of the castle (1643) and drew up the terms of capitulation. In the next century chaplains were probably in residence more or less continuously. It is, in fact, not unlikely that Wardour is one of the few places in England where the "old religion" never ceased to be practised.

In consequence of their recusancy the Arundell family played a somewhat restricted part in political life. Some of its members were, however, implicated in the Great Rebellion, and the third baron, whose part in the sieges of his castle will shortly be described, was subsequently employed by Charles II in diplomatic negotiations. Later still he was one of the "Popish" peers denounced by Titus Oates and spent several years imprisoned in the Tower. Under James II he was restored to grace, sworn of the Privy Council, and appointed to the Privy Seal.

THE CIVIL WAR SIEGES, 1643 AND 1644

The Great Rebellion was characterised by a number of sieges of castles and private houses, some of which were of comparatively small strategic importance but tested the zeal and stamina of the contestants. The two sieges of Wardour were of this class and since they come to mind whenever the castle is mentioned and were marked by outstanding courage on both sides they deserve careful description. They were also responsible for reducing the castle to its present mutilated condition.

In April 1643 Sir Edward Hungerford, the Parliamentarian leader in Wiltshire, who had been campaigning in Somerset, re-entered Wiltshire with 700 horse and foot. His aim was to deprive the leading Royalist families of their houses and property to the enrichment of his own side. The Arundells were strong Royalists and Hungerford accordingly sat down in front of Wardour. Deeming the building strong, however, and its garrison resolute, he called in the aid of Colonel William Strode and his troops. Thus reinforced Hungerford could muster 1300 men and these were pitted against a garrison of twenty-five fighting-men, partly aided and partly hampered by a considerable number of female servants. On 2 May Hungerford called upon the garrison to surrender their persons, their money, and their plate. Thomas, second Lord Arundell, was away in Oxford with the King, and his wife, Blanche, a woman of about sixty, declined to surrender. Thereupon Hungerford brought up two small cannon and for several days battered the castle. Little damage, however, was done beyond smashing a chimney-piece and breaking the windows. The besiegers thereupon proceeded to mine the building, making use for the purpose of the vaults which lay beside or underneath the castle. One of these was designed for the conveyance of beer and fuel, the others formed part of the drainage system and communicated with the privies and with many of the rooms in the castle. One account says that only one mine was sprung, another that two were. However this may be, the fabric was certainly damaged by explosion. This evidently alarmed the garrison, which was very short of sleep, and weakened its morale. Threats by the besiegers to apply petards to the "garden-doors" in order to open up an entrance, to discharge "wild-fire" into the glassless windows, and finally to storm the castle if it were not handed over within a limited time forced the garrison to capitulate on 8 May.

The women and children, who included Arundell's daughter-in-law and grandchildren, were led captive to Shaftesbury. The children, despite their father's plea to Sir William Waller, the Parliamentarian commander, were not restored to liberty but placed under the tuition of a Puritan divine in Essex. The besiegers did much wanton damage. They destroyed many pictures and carried off to Dorchester five cart-loads of hangings and furniture. They also burnt the outhouses, pulled up the palings of the two deer parks, and burnt houses and lodges within them. They felled fine timber and fruit trees and sold them, dug up the heads of twelve fish-ponds and sold the fish at knockdown prices, destroyed the nurseries of the fish, and drove off or sold the horses and cattle. They also cut up and sold the lead piping which carried water into the castle from a source 2 miles (3.2 km) away.

The Parliament was at first undecided whether to destroy the castle or to garrison it. In the end it chose the latter course and put it under the command of Edmund Ludlow, the son of a Wiltshire gentleman, who had joined Hungerford just before the siege. The garrison consisted of Ludlow's own troop of horse and an infantry company. It was immediately challenged by the Royalists, who were planning to send a powerful army into Wiltshire to link up with their forces in Devon. In mid-May Lord Marlborough, one of the Royalist leaders, seized Fonthill House, 4 miles (6.4km) from the castle, in the hope of containing the garrison, but he was driven off by Hungerford. Ludlow destroyed the Royalists' siege-works, sank a well, broke down the vaults, and laid in provisions.

Lord Arundell, the husband of the former defender of the castle, died of wounds a few days after his widow's evacuation, and his son, Henry, the third baron, promptly came up to the castle with a party of cavalry and demanded its surrender. Ludlow refused and Arundell for the time being withdrew. Notwithstanding this, Ludlow's situation was unenviable. The Royalists were strong in the county and the garrisons from which help might be expected to come in the event of a siege were remote. In these circumstances Ludlow's father and some of his friends tried to persuade him not to attempt to stand a siege, and Parliament even empowered him, should he wish, to destroy the fortifications and abandon the castle. To have done so would hardly have been a military disadvantage, but Ludlow judged that the moral effect of clinging on, however desperately, would be considerable. He decided to do this, and to that end visited Southampton to purchase ammunition. He was strengthened in his resolve by finding money, plate and jewels walled up in a cupboard in the castle.

The Royalists, strong as they now were in Wiltshire, were not likely to acquiesce in the retention of Wardour by the Parliament. Moreover Lord Arundell was resolved to recover his property and his home. Before restoring to military measures, however, the Royalists tried to secure the castle by other means. A boy was suborned to offer his services in the kitchen, and, thus introduced within the precincts, proceeded to "poison" some of the ordnance. One of these, an *harquebuz de croq* which stood on the top of the castle, burst asunder. The boy was prevented from doing further mischief, and Ludlow proceeded to add a three-months' stock of provisions to those which he already held by intercepting peasants on their way to Shaftesbury market.

This was the last chance to forage. December had now been reached and the enemy began to invest the castle closely. Under the leadership of Captain Christopher Bowyer they built a breast-work on a hill commanding the castle gate. In addition they tried to persuade Ludlow to surrender. Bowyer was shot immediately after the repudiation of this overture and was succeeded by Colonel Barnes, who built a fort at the distance of a musket-shot from the castle on the hill that surrounded the castle on three sides and took possession of the outhouses of the castle, which had either escaped destruction in May or had been rebuilt since then. These they used as observation posts, though they occupied them effectively only by night. After this, further negotiations were opened by an emissary from Oxford, but were repudiated. The garrison now began to fall short of victuals and had to rely for drink on the castle well, which ran dry each evening. In addition, the portcullis of the main gate was blown up. This forced the garrison to block up the gateway and rely for egress upon a window, since the other entries had been already blocked. The besiegers then tried to undermine the castle wall, but were beaten off with hand grenades.

At the very end of January, if a not very accurate Royalist account may be believed, eleven breaches were made in the walls and a piece of ordnance standing on the leads dislodged. About three weeks after this, as winter was drawing to its close. Sir Ralph Hopton, the Royalist commander in the west, took steps to press the garrison harder by sending reinforcements to the besiegers under the leadership of Sir Francis Doddington. This force seems to have included some Irish "yellow-coats," under the command of Captain Leicester, recently dispatched from Ireland. Though these men played an important part in the final stages of the siege, the force from which they were detached was not wholly reliable; another party of them, which had been ordered to march upon the castle in the preceding November, mutinied when they were as near as Hindon, and marched away. Hopton also sent an engineer and a party of Mendip miners. Mining began and counter-mining was attempted and, on 13 March 1644, Doddington made a further ineffectual appeal to Ludlow to surrender. Next day the vibration caused by one of Ludlow's guns sprang the mine. Ten doors and two of the six angle turrets were blown in and part of the leads blown down. The first-floor room in which Ludlow lodged was severely damaged, three men were killed and part of the garrison's ammunition and corn supply were destroyed. The besiegers, led by Leicester tried to storm, but failed to enter. The chaplain and some other "religious men" thereupon urged Ludlow to surrender. He refused to accept their advice but did not prevent them from making overtures on their own. These, however, were refused and this refusal strengthened the waverers' nerve.

Nevertheless on 16 March hostilities were again suspended and further negotiations initiated. Ludlow now asked to be allowed to march out under arms so as to join the nearest Parliamentary garrison. The request was refused and thereupon the negotiations ended. Considerable unrest, however, developed in the garrison owing to the extreme shortage of food, the precarious state of the fabric and the impending threat of renewed mining. This led to further and final parleys. On 18 March Ludlow left the castle and met Lord Arundell and Doddington outside the garden wall. The Royalist leaders promised that they would try to secure the terms that Ludlow proposed, whereupon Ludlow returned to the castle and ordered his seventy-five men to lay down their arms. However, the terms of the capitulation were not kept, for, though quarter had been promised, two soldiers were executed and the remainder, contrary to another promise, were taken to Oxford. Ludlow himself was treated well. He was indeed imprisoned, but honourably, and was soon afterwards exchanged. This mild treatment was partly due to Arundell, and Ludlow requited his adversary's kindness by revealing to him the whereabouts of the family plate, which the Parliamentarians had buried in a cellar, and by trying, many years later, to prevent the confiscation of the Arundell estates. So ended the second siege of Wardour, which, said a preacher of the day, would ever be "famous to posterity, both for active and passive valour to the utmost."

From an engraving by Samuel and Nathaniel Buck, 1735

Description

In spite of the pronounced Renaissance flavour of the sixteenth-century alterations, Old Wardour Castle is basically the building begun by John, fifth Lord Lovel, who obtained licence to build a castle in 1393. It is not a fortress in the familiar sense of the word "castle." It is rather a tower-house, built for lavish entertainment and domestic comfort, at the same time equipped with some defensive provisions. It belonged to the trend towards greater luxury and ostentation during the course of the fourteenth century when there was no longer the need to make self-protection the first call in English castle building. Nunney Castle, not far away in Somerset, shares this trend, and the pattern continued into the fifteenth century.

The castle stands on a spur within a horseshoe of high ground with the valley opening out towards the west. Insofar as it ever possessed any strategic importance it was capable of controlling the road from Salisbury to the West Country. In plan, Old Wardour is a hexagon, with two towers flanking the entrance on the north-east side breaking the regularity of the figure. Within is a central hexagonal courtyard, little more than a light-well for the rooms looking into it. The bailey, too, is based on a hexagon but with a rectangular northern side in front of the castle entrance. There is nothing else in England like Wardour. For a parallel, one must go to central France to the Château de Concressault in the Department of Cher. This, though on a somewhat larger scale, is also hexagonal in plan with a hexagonal courtyard within. Its outer angles too are surmounted by turrets carried on corbels. The inspiration for Old Wardour clearly came from France, perhaps a result of Lord Lovel's campaigning there during the Hundred Years War.

Unlike many earlier castles where the various rooms and chambers required by a great household were dispersed in towers and often in separate buildings, here at Wardour everything is contained within one mass. The hall, used for state occasions, was placed at first-floor level over the entrance and rose to the full height of the building. At one end of the hall were the service rooms with a great kitchen also at first-floor level. At the other end were the lord's private rooms, solar, chapel and probably a private hall all arranged in two storeys. The remaining two sides of the hexagon were devoted to sets of apartments for the use of guests and perhaps the more senior officers of the household. It is difficult to follow the detailed arrangements of these latter rooms because it is this side of the castle, the south-west, which is the most severely ruined as a result of the Civil War sieges and slighting.

The alterations made by Sir Matthew Arundell after 1570 retained the same domestic planning. His aim was to bring the castle up to date in its decorative style. Although some rearrangement was made in the ground-floor rooms on the south-west side, the main effort was to provide classical-inspired fronts to the main entrance and to the grand approach to the hall, together with a good deal of replacement of the original fenestration with wider if rather uninteresting windows with flat, four-centred arched heads. Particularly on the entrance front there was a determined attempt at symmetrical arrangement of the windows. Fortunately there was no attempt to alter the Perpendicular tracery of those in the hall. This refurbishing of the castle according to advanced taste of the late sixteenth century was designed by the architect, Robert Smythson. Smythson had previously worked on Longleat, not far away and also in Wiltshire.

There was no sustained attempt to put the castle back into a fit state for occupation after the damage of the Civil War. When the Arundells returned at the Restoration they were content to build a small house and other buildings on the south side of the bailey wall. In the early eighteenth century the castle ruins were surrounded by formal gardens. A scheme for restoring the old castle was put forward in 1756 but the construction of New Wardour, designed by James Paine, between 1769 and 1776, settled its future for good. Instead the bailey was laid out in the "picturesque" manner and the grounds about it landscaped and planted. This has given to Old Wardour the flavour of the romantic ruin with its richly contrived setting. It is only when visitors enter the castle that they realise that it was originally a functional building designed for comfortable living at the same time equipped for ostentatious display which accorded with the philosophy of conspicuous waste so favoured by the medieval nobility.

THE EXTERIOR

The bailey

The bailey, or outer courtyard, is very large. Its thin enclosing curtain wall survives for most of the circuit and acts as a retaining wall. The wall belongs to the sixteenth-century alterations but may be on the line of the original curtain. The bailey is entered through an eighteenth-century gateway in the wall on the north. It is possible that a gatehouse

The grotto

may have existed on the west. The Gothic Pavilion or Banqueting House may have been built on its remains. A pair of arches in the basement are bonded into the curtain wall and the plinth of the latter is discontinued between them. Such may be the fragments of an early arched approach. The Pavilion itself, with its emphasis on the gothic ogee arch, was built in the later years of the eighteenth century.

On the left of the present access, behind a line of yews, is a terrace with an elaborate stone, brick and plaster grotto built in 1792 by Josiah Lane of Tisbury, who was a noted builder of rock-work grottoes in Wiltshire. This is part of the eighteenth-century improvements providing fantastically contrived nooks and alcoves. Earlier in the century a bowling green had occupied this spot. On the opposite side, and outside the bailey, are the houses which occupied the interval between Old and New Wardour. Against the curtain wall

Robert Smythson's entrance to the hall

is the ruined shell of the stables built in 1686, and further west is the architecturally distinguished Summer House, perhaps the "Banketting House" built in 1687. Nearby, within the limits of the bailey, is a charming eighteenth-century three-seater closet. Much of its carved panelling and decorative detail survives.

The castle was originally built on the edge of a considerable slope. Ground level within the bailey has been greatly altered. It has been raised by 4ft (1.2m) at the North Tower and 10ft (3m) further west. A good deal of building-up of levels was carried out in the sixteenth century. Two sixteenth-century vaulted cellars built within the curtain wall had windows looking in towards the castle. The sills of these windows are now covered by a metre or more of earth accumulated since.

Trial excavations in 1938 exposed the base of the demolished south-west wall now marked out in the grass and a number of stone-lined drains from the various garderobe shoots all converging into a main drain sloping down towards the lake. It was in this drain, directly under the south wall, that the mine was fired during the seige. Its crater was plainly visible.

The castle

Sufficient remains of the keep or tower-house today for fairly full mental reconstruction. This is helped by its regularity. The towers on either side of the entrance remain almost to full-height. Their purpose was partly defensive as was the machicolation over the wall between them. The corbels for this are still in position. While the precise arrangements of the windows on the other sides cannot be obtained, it is likely that on the ground floor at least they were all simple rect-angular loops giving feeble light to the rooms within but greater security in case of siege. Encircling the wall at the top of the building was a richly decorated cornice with rosettes set in a deep cavetto moulding, while at each of the four angles were turrets carried on bold corbelling. The castle is noted for its excellent masonry using locally quarried Tisbury greensand and some Chilmark limestone for decorative work.

By the end of the sixteenth century in England, defensive preten-sions were largely unnecessary in the greater country houses. The narrow loops were enlarged to increase external lighting for many of the rooms. The replacements, often groups of three mullioned lights, were set as regularly as possible, even to the extent of giving the kitchen blind windows in the wall which carries the main fireplace and flues. The earlier windows remain in the unimportant rooms, such as the ground-floor storage and service quarters and in the garde-robes or latrines, but in the entrance front even these have been suppressed and blocked. So too, on this side, was the original battered plinth, which was cut away and the wall refaced because it clashed with the new style of decorative treatment. It was later much patched with inferior masonry. The entrance front shows the hand of Robert Smythson in the details of the rusticated attached columns of the round-arched entrance and the four, shell-coved niches in austere rectangular classical frames, two on either side of the doorway. The entablature over the entrance has been destroyed and the columns have been cut back to form a chase for a portcullis in front of the door. This was done at the time of the Civil War sieges. The original entrance was equipped with a portcullis but its slot was removed when Sir Matthew Arundell brought the architectural treatment of the main doorway up to date. Above is a long Latin inscription recording the recovery of the property and its restoration to the Arundells. Above this is the Arundell coat of arms in an ornate classical frame and higher still is the bust of Christ in a niche.

THE INTERIOR

Ground floor

The whole ground-floor is raised about 3ft (0.9m) above the present level of the turf outside, in fact to the level of the small terrace in front of the main entrance. Once through the doorway the Renaissance is quickly left behind. The entrance passage was originally vaulted and is of particular interest because it is an early type of fan vaulting. It is in three bays and the vaulting ribs bend stiffly to disappear into the capitals. At the far end of the passage, where it joins the courtyard, the doorway is original and like all the fourteenth-century doorways in the building it has a pointed arch with a relieving arch over it. Within the ogee-moulding of the jamb is a portcullis slot. There was a similar arrangement at the external entrance.

Once inside the courtyard visitors quickly perceive that they are in the hub of the building, the central point being the well. Water was also piped into the castle from outside. From the courtyard much

The coat of arms over the entrance

can be learnt of the domestic planning. According to an inventory of 1605, there were thirty-five rooms of varying size and importance. On either side of the entrance passage were vaulted rooms below the hall. On the left-hand side is the porter's lodge, self-contained with its own garderobe. The porter, through the only door looking into the passage, controlled the entrance. On the same side, and entered from the courtyard, was an unlit storage room. On the other side of the passage was a large room which has now lost its vault. Its floor was lowered in the sixteenth century and a doorway, now blocked, forced through to the cellars to the east. There was a door into it from the courtyard, and it was lit by a now blocked window opposite. It may have served as servants' accommodation or for storage. At the far end was the newel stair which goes up the full height of the tower. Leading off from the bottom of the stair is a doorway into a small storage room. This was connected, in the sixteenth century, with the irregular shaped cellar which gave access to a now blocked underground passage. This passage served as a sally-port and opened out of the south-east side of the bailey wall.

The next opening off the courtyard on the right-hand side of the entrance passage is the splendid formal approach to the hall. This is now one of the "classical" glories of Old Wardour, with its Tuscan columns, simple Doric entablature and lion masks in the spandrels of the arch and on the column bases. The original entrance must also have been distinguished, for at the head of the stairs there remains some ribbed vaulting with a boss of swirling foliage. Further on is the doorway into the room below the great kitchen whose tall lancet-like windows look out into the courtyard. This room also was once vaulted with the ribs springing from geometrical corbels. It may later have been part of the kitchen complex. Certainly there is a large fireplace on the right-hand side which has subsequently been rebuilt, blocking an original door which can be seen in the wall behind. The door in the left corner is the original entrance to the room later converted into a cellar.

Occupying the remainder of this side of the castle, and the whole of the range immediately opposite the entrance, were the four storeys of lodgings; sets of two rooms with the bed-chamber usually having a garderobe leading off it. In modern parlance they might be called flats or apartments and were for guests or senior members of the household. A newel stair provided access. Most of the ground-floor openings have been altered, often by transposing the original dressings from doorway to window and vice-versa. It is, however, possible to see something of the original character even if it is now impossible to determine the functions of the rooms. The partial unblocking of a fourteenth-century window has enabled visitors to see the original cusped, mullioned lights behind.

There was another, but indirect, way of reaching the hall from the courtyard by the doorway on the left-hand, or north-west, side. The actual doorway has been removed from its position to that of a former window; a patch of blocking reveals its site. It gives into a large room which once had a sexpartite, ribbed vault; the corbels and long respond shafts still remain. The room has no fireplace and may have served as an ante-chamber for business functions. It has been suggested that this was the chapel, but other evidence seems to point to the chapel being on the first floor. A long corridor leads off it, from which the stairs to the hall are reached. This corridor had two windows but one was converted in Sir Matthew Arundell's time to an external round-headed doorway opposite the newel stair to the hall.

First floor

Although only the vaulting under the northern end of the hall remains, there is enough to re-create its grandeur for visitors. They stand at the dais end. At the far end are the two doors which open from the buttery and servery into the former screens passage. The position of the wooden screen can be seen in the chases cut into the side walls with a more elaborate recess at floor level to take the heavily moulded sill. Above the screens passage was a gallery, the joist-holes for which are obvious. It was evidently a later development, as the elaborately moulded string course which ran round the room can be seen to have been hacked back at this end to make way for it. The grand stair also opened into the screens passage with steps arranged in the top of the vault. The Gothic pointed arch was cut into a round and given a rectangular frame in order to bring it into line with the other sixteenth-century alterations. The hall was well lighted on each of the long sides by two tall windows filled with fine Perpendicular tracery. Below them are two doorways which serve the two small portcullis chambers in the thickness of the walls. Nearer the dais end was the great fireplace; as it stands now, another sixteenth-century alteration.

The doorway in the corner beside the fireplace leads to the lord's private apartments. These were almost certainly on several floors, and may have spread into the next side of the hexagon. A doorway opens on to a newel stair which begins at first-floor level, and the room beyond, perhaps the parlour, must have been very important. It once had a large window but the only indication of this is the outline of its blocking. Beside it was a fireplace. Perhaps this was where the extraordinary black marble overmantel, valued at £2000 in the seventeenth century and smashed by Parliamentarian troops, was placed. Only fragments of the fireplace have been found, built into the grotto or recovered from the well. At the far end there was connection into another room, another newel stair and a garderobe. Sufficient of the floor above remains to show that another elaborate window opened into the courtyard. High up in the wall is the jamb of a transomed window.

In the wall behind the dais is an inserted sixteenth-century doorway, its round arch decorated with a pellet motif. This opens into what may have been the chapel. It is certain that a chapel existed but its position is less well known. Giving some support to the theory is the presence of carvings on the jambs of this doorway made by recusant Catholics. There are two crosses with INRI above them remaining among the more modern graffiti. They are associated with the names of Mary Diley, John Madgweek and Mould and the date, 1728. Similar recusant crosses are sometimes found on or close to buildings associated with the "old religion." There are the blocked remains of a tall, lancet-like opening on the outer face of the tower. A good deal of alteration was done at this end of the hall at a later date including the blocking of the main newel stair in the North Tower and its realignment to provide a wider approach to the private rooms on the upper floors.

Rather more survives at the service end of the hall although these rooms too are not at present accessible. The stair in the East Tower was probably the main means of communication for the servants, giving on to the screens passage opposite the state entrance. At hall level in the tower was the buttery or pantry. Next to it, its doorway midway along the screens, was the servery equipped with cupboards and a hatch into the kitchen. The kitchen floor has gone but it is still possible to see something of its arrangements. It must have been approached from the screens passage as it was originally securely divided from the chambers beyond. A sixteenth-century door was later cut through. The stair in its north-west angle leads solely to store rooms. There was a massive fireplace occupying the outside wall, with ovens at either end. The flue back is really all that remains. There was another fireplace in the partition wall on the south-west. The kitchen matches the scale of the hall, itself rising up through two storeys.

Beyond the kitchen one of the sets of apartments can be seen. It has had its windows enlarged and some later blocking carried out but it consists of a bed-chamber complete with garderobe and fireplace and a connecting chamber also with a fireplace. Further traces of similar domestic provision can be seen high up in the ruined walls, giving an inkling of the extent and quality of the rooms but insufficient to provide a precise plan.

Printed in Scotland by Her Majesty's Stationery Office at HMSO Press, Edinburgh
Dd 586329 K66 1/78 (14893)